THE ESSENTIAL COLLE

HAYDN

GOLD

Published by
Chester Music Limited
14-15 Berners Street, London W1T 3LJ, UK.

Exclusive Distributors:
Music Sales Limited
Distribution Centre, Newmarket Road, Bury St Edmunds, Suffolk IP33 3YB, UK.
Music Sales Corporation
257 Park Avenue South, New York, NY 10010, USA.
Music Sales Pty Limited
20 Resolution Drive, Caringbah, NSW 2229, Australia.

Order No. CH74580
ISBN 978-1-84772-817-3
This book © Copyright 2008 by Chester Music.

Printed in the EU.

Your Guarantee of Quality:
As publishers, we strive to produce every book to the highest commercial standards.
This book has been freshly engraved and carefully designed to minimise
awkward page turns making playing from it a real pleasure.
Particular care has been given to specifying acid-free, neutral-sized paper
made from pulps which have not been elemental chlorine bleached.
This pulp is from farmed sustainable forests and was produced with
special regard for the environment.
Throughout, the printing and binding have been planned to ensure a sturdy,
attractive publication which should give years of enjoyment.
If your copy fails to meet our high standards, please inform us and
we will gladly replace it or offer a refund.

www.musicsales.com

CHESTER MUSIC
part of The Music Sales Group

London/New York/Paris/Sydney/Copenhagen/Berlin/Madrid/Tokyo

Franz Joseph Haydn

Haydn's family history offers no clues to the huge fame he would achieve during his lifetime as one of the master composers of the Classical era. Franz Joseph Haydn was born on 31st March 1732 into a family of wheelwrights in the Austrian village of Rohrau on the Hungarian border. His roots lay in Hungary, although there is reason to believe that the family had origins in Croatia, which accounts for the Slavonic element in his music.

Haydn's father, himself an amateur musician, encouraged his son's talents. By the age of eight, Franz Joseph had obtained a place in the choir school of St. Stephen's Cathedral in Vienna, where he served as one of the principal soloists and received tuition in harpsichord, violin and organ. At 18, and no longer much use as a choir-boy, Haydn was dismissed and supported himself through teaching, playing the organ in church services and performing in orchestras and string quartets (he would later play occasionally with Mozart in a quartet). He began composing, taking early influence from the powerful 'Sturm and Drang' style of C.P.E. Bach's sonatas.

The turning point of his career came in 1761 when he was appointed to a position in the household of the Esterházys, one of the wealthiest and most influential families in Austria. As Kapellmeister, or music director (1776–90), all the young composer's music belonged to his employer and Haydn was not free to distribute copies. Happily, however, Prince Nikolaus, a lover of music, gave Haydn more than the usual respect reserved for court composers and, with the support of a discerning patron, an excellent orchestra and creative freedom, Haydn flourished: "I could, as head of an orchestra, make experiments, observe what created an impression, and what weakened it, thus improving...and running risks. I was set apart from the world...and so I had to become original."

Works from these early years include around 125 trios for viola, 'cello and *baryton*, a type of viol instrument now obsolete but played by the Prince at the time, and various early comic operas. His output of courtly dances, numbering nearly 400, was similarly prodigious and included the *12 Minuets*. His early string quartets, including the 'Serenade', also provided attractive court entertainment. However, they display maturity in their freshness and deceptive simplicity as Haydn moved away from the stately Baroque and ornamented Rococo styles. This elevation of music from mere entertainment into more original forms is also manifest in his early symphonies, many of which are written in minor keys, including his 'Farewell' Symphony No.45 in F♯ minor. This allowed him to adopt a more serious character in line with German and Austrian trends.

In 1779 Haydn was granted a new contract which allowed him to compose works for other patrons and publish his work. With this newfound freedom, Haydn received commissions from further afield—he wrote a series of Parisian symphonies (1785–86) and was commissioned to write *The Seven Last Words* for Holy Week in Cadiz Cathedral.

Following the death of Prince Nikolaus in 1790, and the succession of a decidedly unmusical new prince, Haydn was granted substantial leave for the first time. With the opportunity to visit the cities where his music was now highly respected, Haydn came to London on two occasions (1791–92 and 1794–95), conducting weekly concerts and premiering new works. His last 12 symphonies were all composed for this trip, including the 'Surprise', 'Military', 'Drumroll' and 'London' Symphony No.104, which was an instant hit, and the 'Oxford' Symphony No.92, performed when he was awarded an honorary Doctorate of Music from Oxford University. Haydn was well received in England, the words of one critic summing up the English admiration: "...it is no wonder that to souls capable of being touched by music, Haydn should be an object of homage, and even of idolatry."

It was at this time that he wrote the most famous of his 29 piano trios—the celebrated *Piano Trio in G major, No.23* with its famous *Gypsy Rondo* finale. The brilliant dance of this last movement is a fine example of Haydn's sense of humour and underlines his Slavonic roots, the piece marked *'all'Ongarese'* (in a Hungarian, or gypsy, style).

Back in Vienna, with yet another new prince in charge and this one eager to restore the musical reputation of the Esterházy family, Haydn resumed work in the household. Under a more relaxed contract, he was to compose a new mass each summer for the Princess's name-day. The six masses he wrote for this purpose, including his most famous and final mass, *Mass in C minor* (1802), are strengthened by his command of symphonic technique. As well as his two oratorios, *The Seasons* and *The Creation* (his biggest choral masterpiece, inspired by having heard Handel in London), he continued to write quartets, including the *'Emperor'*, but he was to write no more symphonies.

Haydn spent the last years of his life in retirement surrounded by the love of friends and the respect of younger musicians. In May 1809, when Napoleon's armies invaded Vienna, Bonaparte himself ordered a guard to be placed outside the composer's home where he lay on his deathbed. He died on 31st May 1809 and at his memorial service two weeks later, Mozart's Requiem was sung in Vienna's Schottenkirche.

In terms of his vocal compositions (oratorios, operas and masses), Haydn heralds the close of an epoch rather than the dawn of a new one, while in his instrumental music (particularly in the genres of the string quartet and the symphony), he is granted the unrivalled position of first great master. He emancipated melody from its confinement to ceremonial courtliness and, infusing it with his native folk music, gave it vitality. Above all, Haydn wrote with directness, simplicity and humour, the following remark he once made about himself being the most revealing: "Anyone can see that I'm a good-natured fellow".

Jessica Maryon-Davies, October 2008

Country Minuet

Composed by Franz Joseph Haydn

Allegro in F major

Composed by Franz Joseph Haydn

Dance in G major

Composed by Franz Joseph Haydn

German Dance

Composed by Franz Joseph Haydn

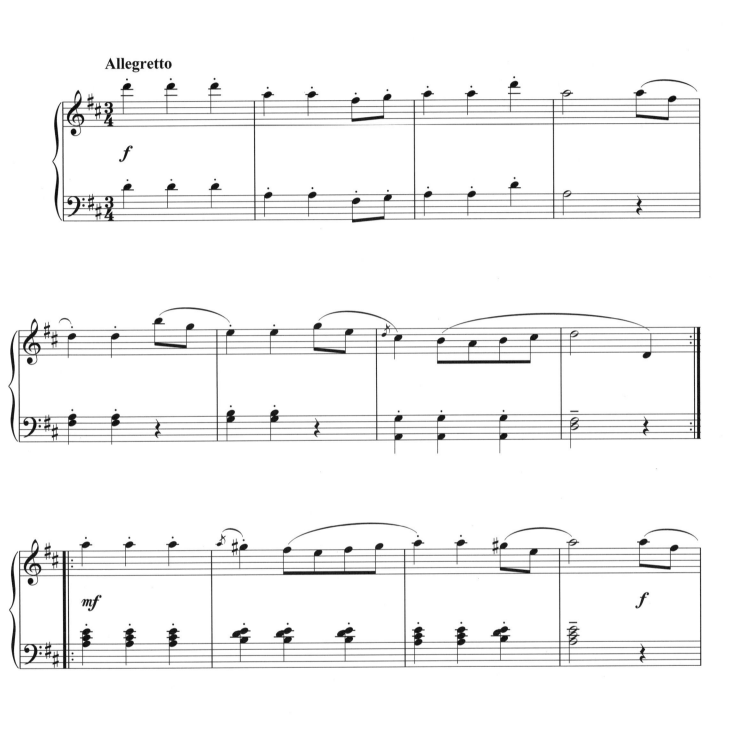

Gypsy Rondo
from 'Piano Trio in G major' Hob.XV:25
(3rd movement)

Composed by Franz Joseph Haydn

Rondo all'ongarese

13

Maggiore

14

Maggiore

Hark! The Mountains Resound!
(Chorus Of Countrymen And Hunters)
from 'The Seasons' Hob.XXI:3

Composed by Franz Joseph Haydn

Allegro vivace

22

The Heavens Are Telling The Glory Of God

from 'The Creation' Hob.XXI:2,

(Part I, No.13)

Composed by Franz Joseph Haydn

Minuet III
from '12 Minuets' Hob.IX:11
(2nd movement)

Composed by Franz Joseph Haydn

Minuet in B♭

Composed by Franz Joseph Haydn

Tempo di Minuetto

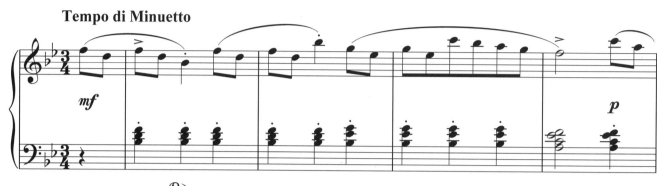

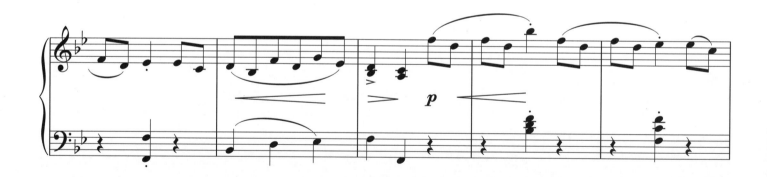

Fine

TRIO

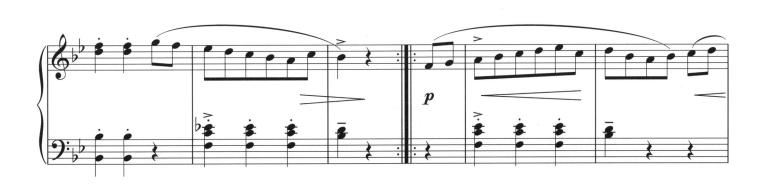

rit. D.C. al Fine

Minuetto Giocoso

Composed by Franz Joseph Haydn

stretto

marcato

Ped.   ✳

D.C. al Fine

Ped.   ✳

34

Piano Sonata No.59 in E♭ major

Hob.XVI:49

(3rd movement: Finale)

Composed by Franz Joseph Haydn

Tempo di Minuetto

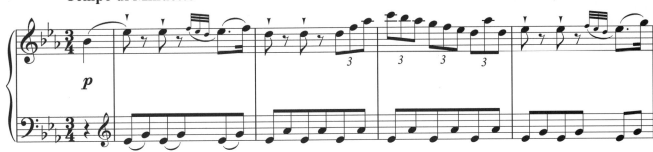

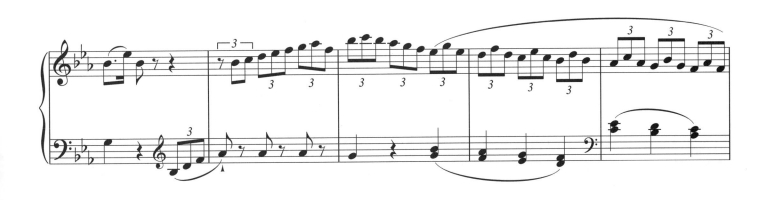

Piano Sonata No.3 in F major

Hob.XVI:9

(3rd movement)

Composed by Franz Joseph Haydn

Piano Sonata No.34 in D major
Hob.XVI:33
(3rd movement)

Composed by Franz Joseph Haydn

Tempo di menuetto

Piano Sonata No.50 in D major
Op.30, No.3 Hob.XVI:37
(3rd movement: Finale)

Composed by Franz Joseph Haydn

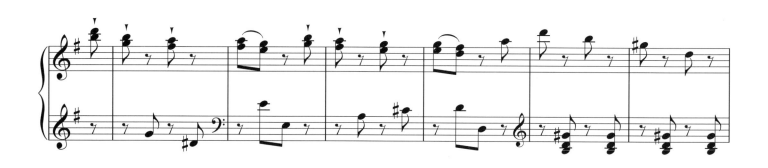

String Quartet in F major, 'Serenade'
Op.3, No.5 Hob.III:17
(2nd movement)

Composed by Franz Joseph Haydn

Andante cantabile

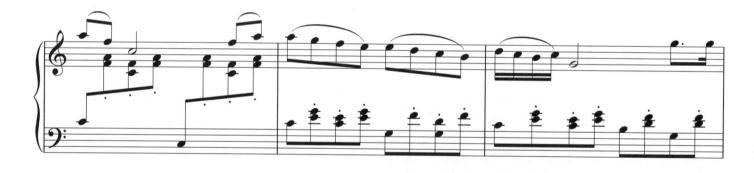

String Quartet Op.51
'The Seven Last Words Of Jesus Christ'
Hob.III:50–56
(Sonata II: Amen dico tibi: hodie mecum eris in paradiso)

Composed by Franz Joseph Haydn

Grave e cantabile

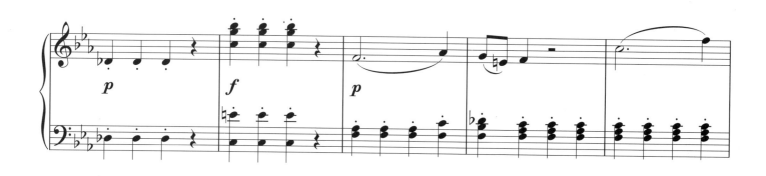

String Quartet No.58 in F major

Op.74, No.2 Hob.III:73

(2nd movement)

Composed by Franz Joseph Haydn

String Quartet No.62 in C major, 'Emperor'

Op.76, No.3 Hob.III:77

(1st movement)

Composed by Franz Joseph Haydn

Allegro

String Quartet No.62 in C major, 'Emperor'

Op.76, No.3 Hob.III:77

(2nd movement: Variations on Theme 'Gott erhalte Franz, den Kaiser')

Composed by Franz Joseph Haydn

Poco adagio, cantabile

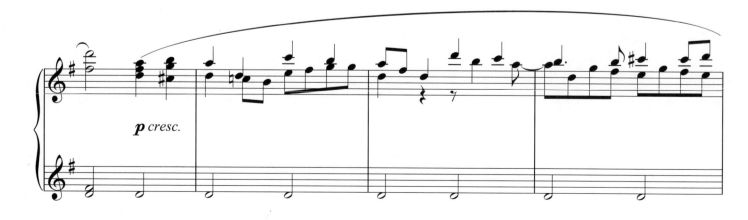

poco più lento

String Quartet No.68 in D minor
Op.103 Hob.III:83
(1st movement)

Composed by Franz Joseph Haydn

Andante grazioso

Symphony No.45 in F♯ minor, 'The Farewell'

Hob.I:45

(1st movement)

Composed by Franz Joseph Haydn

Allegro assai

Symphony No.92 in G major, 'The Oxford'

Hob.I:92

(2nd movement)

Composed by Franz Joseph Haydn

Adagio

Symphony No.94 in G major, 'The Surprise'

Hob.I:94

(2nd movement)

Composed by Franz Joseph Haydn

Andante

Symphony No.97 in C major

Hob.I:97

(2nd movement)

Composed by Franz Joseph Haydn

Adagio ma non troppo

Symphony No.100 in G major, 'The Military'

Hob.I:100

(2nd movement)

Composed by Franz Joseph Haydn

Symphony No.101 in D major, 'The Clock'

Hob.I:101

(2nd movement)

Composed by Franz Joseph Haydn

Andante

Symphony No.103 in E♭ major, 'The Drumroll'

Hob.I:103

(3rd movement)

Composed by Franz Joseph Haydn

Tempo di Menuetto

D.C. al Fine

Symphony No.104 in D major, 'The London'
Hob.I:104
(2nd movement)

Composed by Franz Joseph Haydn

Andante

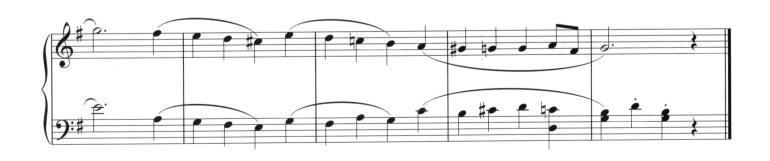

Symphony No.104 in D major, 'The London'

Hob.I:104

(3rd movement)

Composed by Franz Joseph Haydn

Tempo di Minuetto

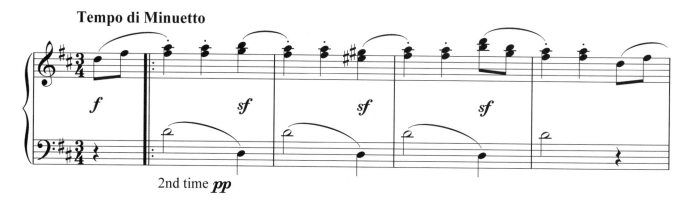

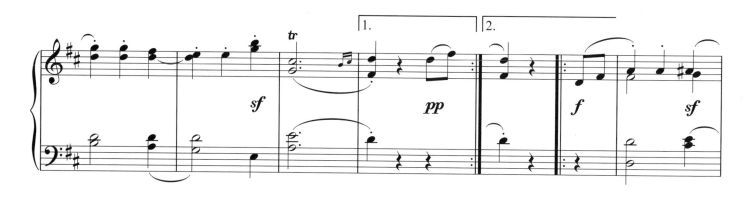

TRIO

D.C. al Fine

123456789

If you like this book you will also like these...